Stay Healthy!

Why Do We Need to Drink Water?

Angela Royston

Heinemann Library
Chicago, Illinois

Photo research by Ruth Blair, Ginny Stroud-Lewis
Designed by Jo Hinton-Malivoire, bigtop
Printed and bound in China by South China Printing Company

10 09 08 07 06
10 9 8 7 6 5 4 3 2 1

Library of Congress Cataloging-in-Publication Data
Royston, Angela.
  Why do we need to drink water? / Angela Royston.
       p. cm. -- (Stay healthy)
  Includes bibliographical references and index.
  ISBN 1-4034-7608-X (library binding-hardcover) -- ISBN 1-4034-7613-6
(pbk.)   1. Water in the body--Juvenile literature. I. Title. II. Series.
  QP535.H1R6954 2006
  612'.01522--dc22
                                              2005010380

Acknowledgments
The author and publisher are grateful to the following for permission to reproduce copyright material:
Corbis pp.4, 20(Norbert Schaefer); p.5(Richard T. Nowitz) p.14(Gabe Palmer); Getty Images pp.6, 18(Stone), pp.7, 23b(Digital Vision), p.15, pp.19, 23a, 23c(Photodisc); Harcourt Education pp.8, 9, 12(Gareth Boden), pp.11, 13, 16, 17, 21, 22 (Tudor Photography); Science Photo Library p.10.

Cover photograph of boy with water spout reproduced with permission of Corbis. Back cover images reproduced with permission of Harcourt Education/ Gareth Boden and Tudor Photography.

Every effort has been made to contact copyright holders of any material reproduced in this book. Any omissions will be rectified in subsequent printings if notice is given to the publisher.

The author and publisher would like to thank Dr. Sarah Schencker, Dietitian, for her comments in the preparation of this book.

Some words are shown in bold, **like this.** You can find them in the picture glossary on page 23.

Contents

Why Do You Get Thirsty?

You feel thirsty when your body needs more water.

Your mouth goes dry.

When you drink, you give your body the water it needs.

Why Do You Need to Drink?

Your body loses water every day.

Pee, **sweat**, and tears are mostly water.

Blood and **mucus** are mostly water.

When you drink, you put back the water you lose.

Do Drinks Have Water in Them?

All drinks have water in them.

Most drinks are water mixed with other things.

Most fizzy drinks also have sugar in them.

Water is the best drink to have!

Does Food Have Water in It?

All food has some water in it.

Fruit and vegetables have the most.

Oranges are full of juice.

Do you know how to make orange juice?

Making Orange Juice!

1. Ask an adult to cut four large oranges in half.

2. Using a juicer, squeeze each half.

3. Pour the orange juice into a glass.

4. Enjoy drinking your fresh orange juice!

When Do You Need to Drink Most?

You need to drink most when you are hot.

You **sweat** more when you are hot.

When you sweat, you lose
more water.

How Do You Lose the Most Water?

You lose most water when you pee.

You should pee several times a day.

Pee is one way your body gets rid of waste.

Do not forget to wash your hands afterwards!

What Happens If You Do Not Drink Enough?

If you do not drink enough water, you will get **dehydrated**.

If you get dehydrated, you might get a headache.

Drinking some water might help.

Keep Drinking!

Drink two glasses of water.

Drink two more glasses of water an hour later. What happens?

You should need to go to
the toilet.

But you should also feel more
lively and healthy.

How Much Do You Need to Drink?

You should drink four glasses a day.

Drink more if you are very active.

Glossary

 **dehydrated**   not having enough water

 **mucus**   kind of liquid made inside your body. Snot is a kind of mucus.

 **sweat**   salty water made by your body. Sweat comes out through your skin.

Index

Note to Parents and Teachers

Reading nonfiction texts for information is an important part of a child's literacy development. Readers can be encouraged to ask simple questions and then use the text to find the answers. Most chapters in this book begin with a question. Read the questions together. Look at the pictures. Talk about what the answer might be. Then read the text to find out if your predictions were correct. To develop readers' inquiry skills, encourage them to think of other questions they might ask about the topic. Discuss where you could find the answers. Assist children in using the contents page, picture glossary, and index to practice research skills and new vocabulary.